RBT
COLORING BOOK

I AM A BEHAVIOR TECHNICIAN

IT'S MY JOB TO JUDGE YOU

Published by Aayushais Tripathi Publishing

RBT
NUTRITION FACTS

AMOUNT PER SERVING: **1 AWESOME RBT**

	% DAILY VALUE**
HARD WORK	1000%
LAZINESS	0%
TALENT	500%
PASSION	100%
DEDICATION	300%
CAFFEINE	110%

*Percentage daily values are based on your unique diet

I AM A YOUNG ILLUSTRATOR FOCUSED ON CREATING QUALITY COLORING BOOKS. YOUR FEEDBACK IS CRUCIAL FOR ME. SO PLEASE DO CONSIDER LEAVING ME A REVIEW ON AMAZON.

BEING A BEHAVIOR TECHNICIAN CAN BE STRESSFUL. I HOPE THIS BOOK HELPED YOU IN SOME WAY OR FORM.

!!!THANK YOU FOR PURCHASING THIS BOOK!!!

!!WISH YOU A VERY HAPPY FUTURE AHEAD!!